EAU CLAIRE DISTRICT LIBRARY
6528 East Main Street
P.O. Box 328
EAU CLAIRE, MI 49111

W9-AKE-259

Ladders

My Body

World Book

in association with

EAU CLAIRE DISTRICT LIBRARY

T 137500

World Book, Inc.
233 N. Michigan Ave.
Chicago, IL 60601
in association with Two-Can Publishing.

For information about other World Book publications, visit our
Web site http://www.worldbook.com or call 1-800-WORLDBK
(967-5325). For information about sales to schools and libraries,
call 1-800-975-3250 (United States); 1-800-837-5365 (Canada).

Written by: Angela Wilkes
Story by: Sue Barraclough
Consultants: Dr. Iram Siraj-Blatchford, Institute of Education, London;
             Anita de Brouwer, Eureka! The Museum for Children, Halifax
Editor: Sarah Fecher
Art director: Belinda Webster
Design: Alex Frampton
Main illustrations: Rhian Nest James
Computer illustrations: Jon Stuart
U.S. editor: Sharon Nowakowski

2006 Printing
© Two-Can Publishing, 1998

All rights reserved. No part of this publication may be reproduced,
stored in a retrieval system, or transmitted in any form or by any
means electronic, mechanical, photocopying, recording, or otherwise,
without written permission from the publisher.

"Two-Can" is a trademark of Two-Can Publishing.

Library of Congress Cataloging-in-Publication Data

Wilkes, Angela.
     My body / Angela Wilkes.
          p.   cm. — (Ladders)
     Includes index.
     Summary: Describes the various parts of the human body and the jobs that each part performs
while also suggesting ways to care for the body and keep it well.
     ISBN 0-7166-7709-1 (hc) – ISBN 0-7166-7710-5 (sc)
     1. Body, Human—Juvenile literature. 2. Human anatomy—Juvenile literature.
     [1. Body, Human. 2. Human anatomy.] I. Title. II. Series.
     QM27.W55 1998
     612—dc21   98-16282

Photographic credits: p4: Julian Cotton Photo Library; p6: The Stock Market; p7: The Stock Market;
p8: The Photographers Library; p9: Julian Cotton Photo Library; p10: Tony Stone Images;
p11: Tony Stone Images; p14: The Stock Market; p16: Lupe Cunha; p17: The Stock Market;
p19: Images Colour Library; p20: Britstock-IFA; p21: Tony Stone Images; p22: Telegraph Colour Library;
p23: Julian Cotton Photo Library.

Printed in China

7 8 9 10 09 08 07 06

What's inside?

This book tells you lots of exciting things about your body. Inside your body, you have soft parts and hard parts that all do special jobs. They work together to help you speak and move, eat and drink, play and sleep!

My body

Your body is amazing! It's made up of lots of different parts inside a stretchy covering of skin. Girls and boys look different from each other but their bodies work in the same ways. Can you name the main parts of your body?

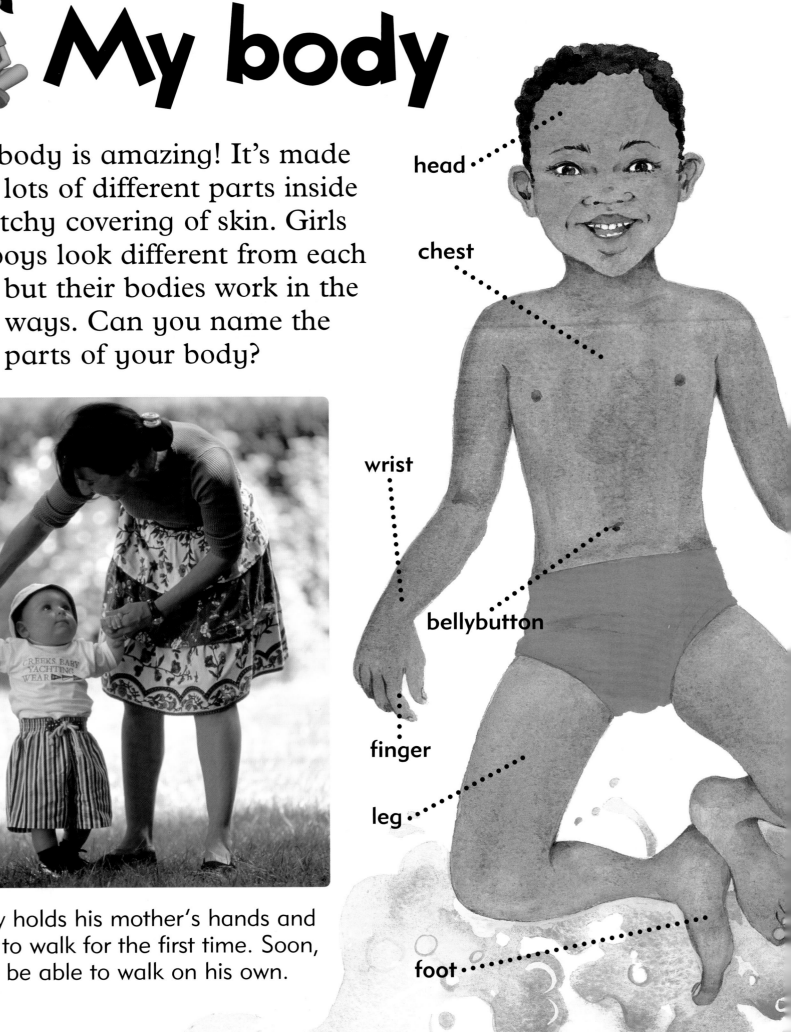

head

chest

wrist

bellybutton

finger

leg

foot

A baby holds his mother's hands and learns to walk for the first time. Soon, he will be able to walk on his own.

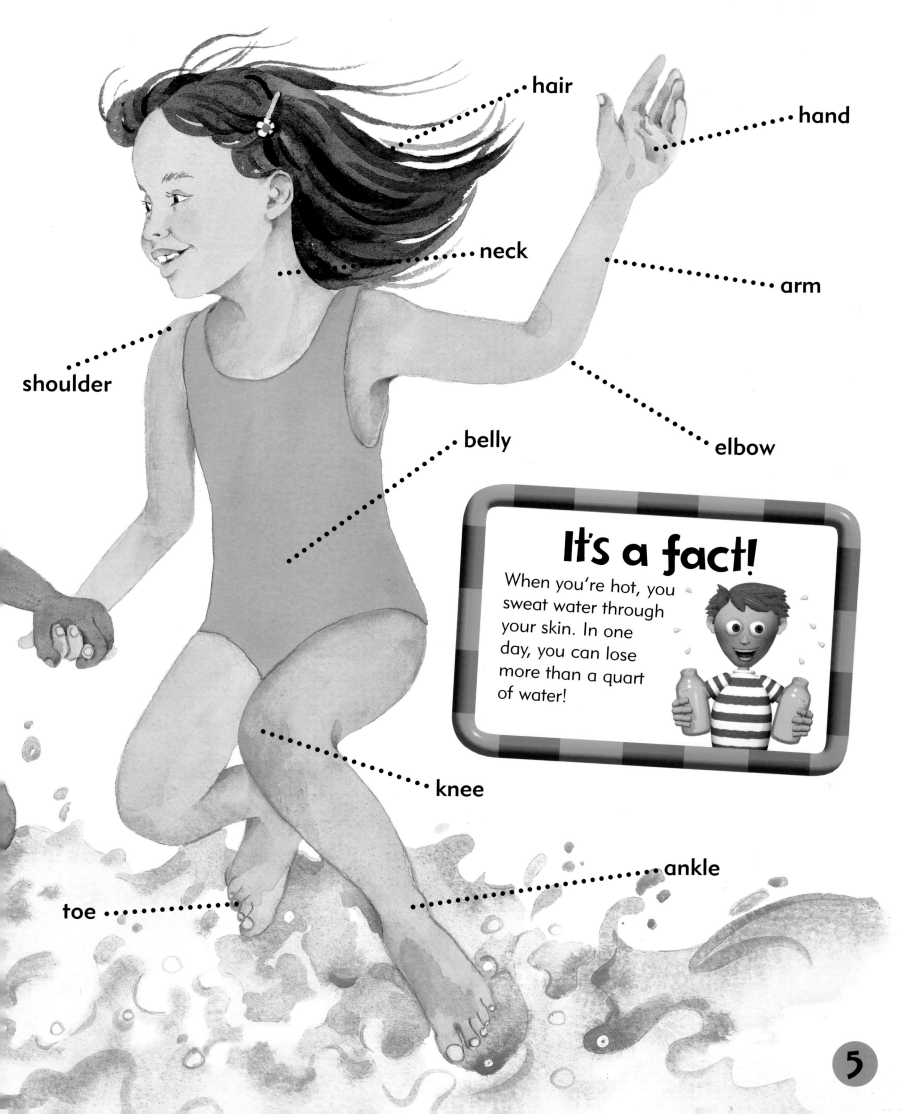

hair

hand

neck

arm

shoulder

belly

elbow

It's a fact!

When you're hot, you sweat water through your skin. In one day, you can lose more than a quart of water!

knee

toe

ankle

5

Bones

Inside your body, you have more than 200 hard bones that are different shapes and sizes. Together they make a big, strong frame, called a skeleton. Try tapping your knee. Can you feel a bone underneath your skin?

Your **skull** is a bony case that protects your brain.

Two rows of curved **ribs** make a large cage around your heart and lungs.

Your **backbone**, or spine, is made up of lots of little bones, like beads on a string.

These skaters are rolling quickly along a path. They wear helmets and pads to protect their bones if they fall.

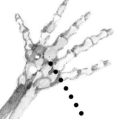

Three long, straight arm bones join at your **elbow**.

There are more than 25 **hand bones** in your palm, wrist, and fingers.

Your **hip bones** join your legs to the rest of your body.

Your **kneecap** protects the joint where your leg bones meet.

The longest and strongest bone in your body is your top **leg bone**.

Luckily, broken bones are easy to mend. A doctor wraps them in a stiff plaster cast, then they grow together again.

It's a fact!

Lots of animals have bones inside their bodies. Dogs and cats have skeletons, and so do tiny fish!

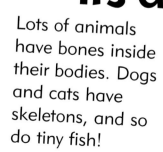

Muscles

Strong muscles under your skin help you bend and stretch your body. You use muscles every time you shake your head, wiggle a toe, or jump up and down. The big picture shows children playing leapfrog. This game uses lots of muscles!

It's a fact!

Exercise makes your muscles stronger. Some people make their muscles so strong, they can lift a car!

Dancing is a really fun way to exercise. Everybody has a good time moving their arms and legs to music!

Bend your back and try to curl up into a round ball.

Pull your knees up toward your head.

Run and jump over your friend! Use the muscles in your arms to **push** yourself over.

With lots of practice, your body can do amazing things. This girl can jump up high and stretch her legs wide apart.

As you jump, **stretch** out your legs, ready to land on the ground.

To keep your head safe, **tuck** it under your hands.

Inside my body

Your body is packed full of soft parts, called organs, that do extremely important jobs. They help you to breathe, to eat, and even to think. There's also a lot of thick blood inside your body. It carries food around, from your head to your toes!

Your **brain** is inside your head. It helps you to think and learn.

When you breathe out underwater, you can see the air come out of your mouth and nose in lots of bubbles!

Every time you breathe in, two spongy bags, called **lungs**, fill up with air.

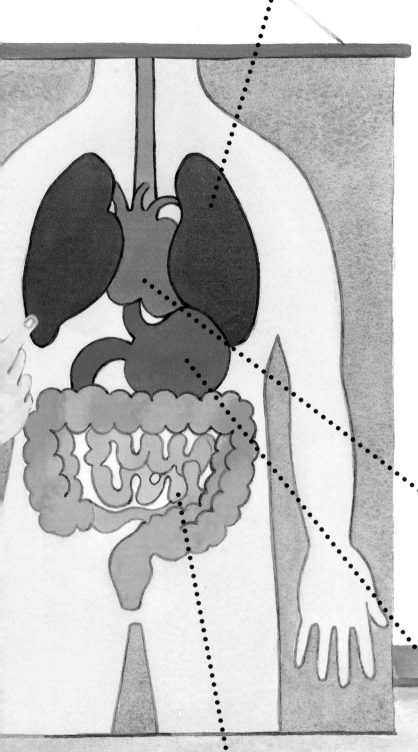

Doctors use a special instrument to listen to your heart beating inside your chest. Your heart sounds like a drum. Thump! Thump!

Your **heart** pumps blood around your body all day and all night.

Your **stomach** churns up all the food you eat into a mushy soup!

Your wiggly **gut** soaks up the best bits of food. The rest of it slides to the end and you go to the bathroom!

Playing in the park

The park is full of children playing different games. They bend and stretch their bodies in all sorts of ways!

12

Words you know

Here are words that you read earlier in this book. Say them out loud, then find the things in the picture.

knee   **elbow**   **leg**

shoulder   **chest**   **arm**

EAU CLAIRE DISTRICT LIBRARY

 # My face

Everyone's face is different! Your face is the part of your body that shows people how you feel inside. Crying can mean that you are feeling sad. Smiling shows everyone that you are happy.

Lots of **eyelashes** help stop specks of dirt from getting into your eyes.

When you are happy, your **mouth** curls up into a big smile!

Your **chin** is at the very bottom of your face.

These brothers are identical twins. They were born on the same day and look almost exactly the same as each other.

Your **forehead** may wrinkle when you are mad.

Some **cheeks** turn rosy when they are warm.

Your **nose** tells you if a smell is nice or nasty.

Strong, rock-hard **teeth** are for biting and chewing food.

It's a fact!

If you do not cut your hair, it may keep growing until it trails behind you on the ground!

15

See and hear

All day long, you look at things around you and hear all sorts of sounds. You do it without even trying! The children in the big picture are singing as they read and play music. Do you like listening to music?

You can hear soft sounds and loud sounds with your **ears**.

This girl is wearing **glasses** to help her see more clearly.

These deaf children are talking with their hands. They can't hear words so they make special signs that stand for words.

You use your **eyes** to look at the world around you.

When you look through a magnifying glass, everything seems really big—even the patterns on a little butterfly's wings.

It's easy to **sing** along to the music when you know the words.

As you **listen** to a tune, try to clap your hands in time.

Touch and feel

Does a feather feel soft or hard, smooth or rough? You find out how things feel by touching them. Your fingertips are best for touching but toes are good, too. The big picture shows lots of things you can find on a beach. Can you imagine how they feel?

When you dig your feet into sand, the tiny grains **tickle** between your toes.

Rock is hard and jagged. It feels **rough** against your bare skin.

It's a fact!

Your body hates to be cold. When it gets too cold, your nose and cheeks turn red, or even blue!

Seaweed feels **slimy** when it's wet. It slips through your fingers.

This boy loves his pet dog. He presses his face against the dog's soft, furry coat to give him a big hug.

On a hot day, it feels good to dip your hand in the **cool** seawater.

Keep away from a sea urchin or it will sting you with its **prickly** spines!

Taste and smell

Your tongue does a special job. When you eat, it tells you if your food tastes nice or yucky. Your nose helps, too, by catching smells that float into the air. The smell of fresh popcorn or hot pizza can make you feel really hungry.

Licking an ice cream makes your tongue tingle. It feels cold in your mouth but tastes yummy!

Lemons taste so **sour** that eating them makes your face pucker!

Cookies and cakes are baked with lots of sugar to make them taste **sweet**.

Salty chips and peanuts can make you thirsty.

Steaming hot pizza **smells** so good that you can't wait to eat it.

A fresh flower smells lovely. Holding it close to your nose is the best way to sniff its special scent.

21

Keeping well

Your body is a wonderful machine—just think of all the things it can do. But you must take care of it to stay healthy. You need plenty of exercise, water, fresh food, and sleep. You need to wash each day to keep yourself clean!

Brush your teeth with **toothpaste** to help them stay clean and white.

Fresh fruit is tasty and good for you too. It helps your body grow.

Soap is for washing your skin. You rub it all over—even behind your ears!

If you cut your skin, wear a **bandage** to keep it clean while it mends.

Shampoo gets rid of the dirt in your hair and makes lots of bubbles, too!

Soft, thick **pajamas** keep you warm and cozy when you curl up in bed.

Playing can tire you out. A short nap gives your body a rest, so that you are ready to start all over again.

Fun at the beach

On a hot day, lots of people go to the beach. It's fun to play on the warm sand and to splash in the water.

24

Words you know

Here are some words that you read earlier in this book. Say them out loud, then find the things in the picture.

mouth   eyes   nose

teeth   chin   ears

Life Guard

What are some of the sounds the children could be hearing?

Which yummy icy food makes your tongue tingle?

Sam's big surprise

Sam was 5 years old. He liked to do all kinds
of fun things, but he had one pet hate,
and that was...waiting!

When Dad baked a cake, as soon as Sam smelled it, he asked, "Is it ready yet?"

And when Sam found out that he had to wait, his face turned bright red and he shouted, "I *can't* wait!"

When Mom took Sam to his cousins', as soon as his house was out of sight, Sam asked, "Are we there yet?"

And when Sam found out that he had to wait, his face turned bright red and he shouted, "I *can't* wait!"

One day, Mom said that she was going to have a baby. Sam was very excited, but he did not like waiting for the baby. He would gently put his hand on Mom's tummy to feel the baby kicking inside!

Every day, he asked, "Will the baby be born today?" but Mom just smiled at him and said, "Remember, Sam, sometimes you have to wait."

And guess what Sam shouted then?!

One morning, Sam found Dad packing a bag.

"We're going to the hospital," said Dad, "the baby will be born today."

The second Sam heard this, he raced down the stairs and jumped up and down. "When will you be home?" asked Sam.

just lie in their cribs, so they need things to look at."

Sam sat down and opened up a magazine that lay on the floor. It was full of pictures of soft, colorful things.

"Wow!" shouted Sam, pointing at a picture of a huge mobile. There were lots of paper airplanes dangling from strings. "Do we have one of these?" he asked.

"Oh no," said Grandma, "but we have lots of other things." She pulled a baby's rattle out of a box and gave it a shake.

Then, he found out that he had to wait. His face turned bright red, and he shouted, "I *can't* wait!"

"This is worth waiting for," said Mom, and gave him a big hug.

"Be good," called Dad, as they hurried to the car.

Sam watched Mom and Dad drive away. "I *can't* wait," he mumbled to himself and his face turned redder.

Sam heard lots of noise, so he went to look for Grandma and Grandpa. He found them in the baby's nursery.

"While we wait," said Grandma, "we'll get the baby's room ready. When babies are small, they can't run and play like you do, Sam. Their muscles aren't even strong enough for them to hold up their own heads. Most of the time, babies

27

"What is he up to?" wondered Grandpa, watching him go into his bedroom and shut the door.

"Search me!" said Grandma.

A little while later, Grandpa was painting animal shapes on the nursery door. He tiptoed across the landing and tapped on Sam's bedroom door.

"I was just wondering if your door needed painting, too," said Grandpa.

"No, but can I have some paint?" asked Sam.

Grandpa gave Sam the can of paint, and Sam said thank you. Then he went back into his bedroom and closed the door.

Sam stayed in his room all afternoon. He came out only when it was time for dinner. He had sticky tape in his hair, paint on his chin, and pieces of string hanging off his shoulders and chest.

"Look at the mess you're in!" said Grandma. "What have you been doing?"

Sam just grinned and said, "It's a big surprise."

Not long after it got dark, the telephone rang— Grandma and Grandpa raced to answer it. It was Dad calling to say that Sam had

"Can I have the box?" asked Sam.

"What for?" replied Grandma.

"Just to play with," said Sam.

Later on, Sam watched Grandpa reaching and stretching. He was hanging a long, brightly colored border all around the room. It had lots of pictures for the baby to look at.

"Can I have some tape?" asked Sam.

"What for?" asked Grandpa.

"It's a surprise," said Sam.

And with that, he bent down and lifted up the box with the magazine, tape, and some string and hurried out of the nursery.

a little baby sister and that they were coming home in the morning.

As soon as Sam heard that he had a sister, his face turned red, he jumped up and down, and he shouted, "I *can't* wait to see her!"

"It won't be long," said Grandma, "but now it's time for bed. You must be tired."

Sam put on his pajamas, then he brushed his teeth and washed his face. He climbed into bed and Grandpa and Grandma gave him a hug, then they turned out the light. A minute later, Sam tiptoed out of his room, holding something in his hands. He disappeared into the nursery for a moment, then crept back into his bedroom.

The next morning, Sam was standing at the window, waiting for Mom and Dad to arrive with his new sister.

"They're here, they're here!" shouted Sam when he spotted the car.

Sam flung open the door and his dad came in holding the tiny bundle in his arms. He bent down to show Sam.

Sam saw a little red face, with tightly closed eyes, and two little pink, wrinkled hands that were opening and closing.

Sam couldn't believe how tiny the baby's hands were compared to his. She had tiny, pink fingernails too, and tiny eyelashes, and a little bit of hair. Her skin was the softest thing that Sam had ever felt.

"She looks angry," said Sam, peering at his sister's crumpled face.

"She looks just like you do when you shout you can't wait," laughed Dad.

"Will you bring her upstairs?" asked Sam. "We have a surprise for her."

29

Everyone went upstairs, and Sam pushed open the nursery door.

Mom and Dad were amazed to see the colorful borders around the room, the animal paintings on the door, and all the baby toys. But most of all, they admired a large mobile that was hanging next to the crib.

"So that's what you were doing all day," said Grandpa. "You were making a surprise present for your new sister!"

"Oh," said Mom, "it looks beautiful, Sam. Thank you very much."

"It must have taken you a long time to make!" said Dad.

By now, the baby was yawning so Mom gently put her in the crib and sang her a lullaby.

"Well, was she worth waiting for?" asked Dad.

"Oh yes," said Sam. "Can I hold her?"

"Wait until she wakes up from her nap," said Mom.

When she said that, Sam's face started to turn red. But he suddenly realized he might wake and frighten his sister if he shouted his usual, "I *can't* wait!"

"I *can* wait," Sam whispered as he smiled and thought of all the fun he would have with his new sister.

Puzzles

Double trouble!

These two pictures are not exactly the same. Can you find the four things that are different in picture b?

a

b

Close-up!

We've zoomed in on some children you have seen in this book. Can you figure out what they're doing?

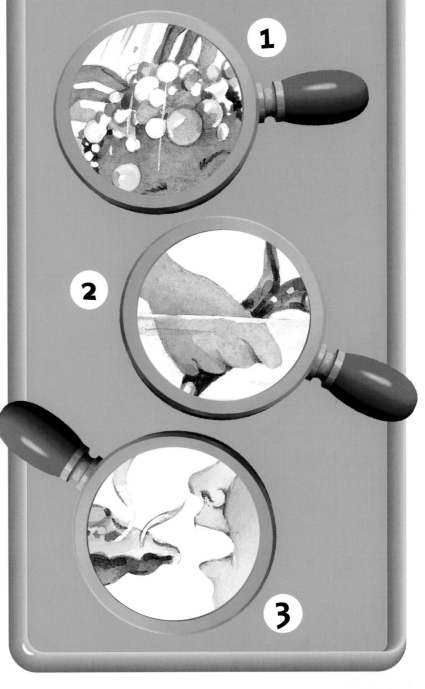

Answers: **Double trouble!** both legs bent, curly hair, shoe missing, glasses; **Close-up!** 1 washing hair, 2 feeling seaweed and water, 3 smelling and eating pizza.

Index

True or false quiz

Can you figure out who is telling the truth? Turn to the page numbers listed to help you find the answers.

1 When you're hot, you sweat water through your skin. **Go to page 5.**

2 If you do not cut your hair, it may grow until it trails on the ground. **Go to page 15.**

3 Some people are so strong, they can lift an airplane. **Go to page 8.**

4 When you feel cold, your nose turns green! **Go to page 18.**

Answers: 1 true, 2 true, 3 false, 4 false.

EAU CLAIRE DISTRICT LIBRARY

EAU CLAIRE DISTRICT LIBRARY